ENTERING INTO THE MIND OF GOD

ANTHONY PHILLIPS

Illustrated with sculptures by Michael Finn

Photographs by Bob Berry

Published in Great Britain in 2002 by
Society for Promoting Christian Knowledge
Holy Trinity Church
Marylebone Road
London NW1 4DU

British Library Cataloguing-in-Publication Data

A catalogue record for this book is available
from the British Library

ISBN 0–281–05512–2

Typeset by Pioneer Associates, Perthshire
Printed in Singapore

Contents

In memory of
Michael and Cely Finn
with love and gratitude

Preface

This book is an expanded version of my addresses at the traditional three-hour Good Friday service held at Truro Cathedral in April 2000. My purpose was to discover what was involved for the disciple who willed to obey Jesus' command to take up his cross and follow him. I explored this by inviting the congregation to make the traditional seven words from the cross their own, and so enter into the mind of God at this moment of supreme love for his creation.

Michael Finn's crucifixes confront the onlooker with the same challenge and complement and strengthen the text. Both word and image make abundantly clear the bleakness of the cross, the harshness of what discipleship must of necessity involve.

Sadly, Michael Finn died on Palm Sunday 2002, the day of crosses. He had read the text and was delighted that he could share in the project. His work had led him into the mystery of the cross, which he embraced with an artist's passion. In doing so, he enabled others to reach a more profound understanding of the crucifixion born out of his own deep faith.

Anthony Phillips
Cornwall, April 2002

Introduction

In his first letter to the Corinthians, Paul proclaims that when he preached the gospel to them, he decided to know nothing 'except Jesus Christ and him crucified' (1 Corinthians 2.2) –

> a stumbling block to Jews and folly to Gentiles, but to those who are called, both Jews and Greeks, Christ the power of God and the wisdom of God. For the foolishness of God is wiser than men, and the weakness of God is stronger than men. (1 Corinthians 1.23–5)

As a result, throughout 2,000 years of faith, the cross has become the symbol of Christian belief – a hideous instrument of torture upon which God in his foolishness and weakness allowed people to do their worst.

To this day, Christians mark the new believer with this sign. In doing so, they show that the baptized has also passed from death to life, is part of the community of the resurrection. But the signing indicates that that community can be only what the cross makes it, by fully appropriating for itself that very sign with which each member has been marked. As the Saviour made clear, true disciples have no option but to take up their cross and follow.

It was only after Calvary that his command became intelligible, that the cost of discipleship was laid bare. Yet we try and avoid its naked brutality, take the body down, clean the demonic instrument of death, and wear it round our necks for safety. But it is the most unsafe sign in all the world, for its signifies our willingness to be stripped and torn apart, stretched until we have nothing left to offer, until we can say, 'It is finished.'

For one day in the year, Good Friday, Christians are invited to enter into the physical agony of the cross as Our Lord entered into it, to follow him in his pain and isolation from both God and humankind, until in faith he surrendered his life to his Creator, as at some time in our uncertain future we all must do. Here in the mystery of his naked vulnerability, we see most clearly the mind of God, for Jesus does not die in silence.

As he moves towards this final offering of the love that he is, words are uttered – words that betray his thoughts and feelings as he endures his inexplicable final incarnate hours. If we too are to take up that bloodied instrument of death – allow, as we must, our body to be broken with his body, our blood to flow with his blood – then we must listen anew to these final words of the Saviour. For in taking up our cross these words become our words too.

The seven words of the dying Jesus come from different Gospels. Matthew (27.46) and Mark (15.34) have one word in common; Luke (23.34; 23.43; 23.46) and John

(19.26–7; 19.28; 19.30) both have three unique to each of their Gospels. Inevitably this raises questions of their authenticity. Why should the Gospels record different sayings? Can they be regarded as the actual words of Jesus?

We need to remember that all the Gospels were written long after the events they purport to describe. Nor were the evangelists recording these events as a modern historian would, but as theologians interpreting them to their contemporary church in order to instruct and strengthen them. Because each evangelist faced a different situation in the audience for whom he wrote, he selected his material to fit his particular theology. For instance, Luke's words take up his Gospel's theme of forgiveness and repentance.

We have then not one but four distinctive accounts of the passion narrative which, if we attempt to harmonize, does violence to the text. While each of the evangelists drew on the traditions available, all were anxious that in creating their own picture of the crucified Jesus they should enable their specific Christian audience to identify with him and the God he called his Father.

We should then, as we do with Michael Finn's different representations of the crucifixion, count ourselves fortunate that in our Scriptures we have varied accounts of the passion of Our Lord. While we can no longer determine how much is interpretation rather than fact, they all show Jesus surrendering himself to his now inevitable yet incomprehensible death in total impotence, an impotence he wills his followers to embrace.

For those who gave us our Gospels, the final words they chose to put into the mouth of the dying Saviour are then of singular importance. We need not worry that they come from different Gospels. They all reflect the evangelists' understanding of Jesus' most intimate thought as he irrevocably expressed his commitment to his people, showed as God could show in no other way, that he is love and can be no other.

So in making these final words from the cross our own, we enter directly into the mind of God at his most vulnerable. His words are not just particular expressions uttered at this defining moment of all history but the gracious outpouring of himself that once given can never be withdrawn. The words continue to spend and be spent on those who appropriate them for themselves, enabling them to follow where he has gone before, both in utter degradation and to ultimate glory.

Let us then meditate on those seven words in the order in which the Church has traditionally done so, for they provide the most profound insight into what it means to take up our cross and follow. As Jesus' arms stretched on their wooden board will to embrace us despite the restraining nails, and as in thankfulness we allow them to do so, let us make his words our words and discover the cost and the joy of a love we would make our own.

Blessed Saviour, who in your hours of desolation
hung upon the cross, stretching forth your
loving arms:
embrace us in those arms, that your cross
may be our cross;
so that we may embrace all who are desolate and
for whom
you died and rose again, that all people may
live like you
in the image and likeness of your Father,
to whom with you and
the Holy Spirit be glory for ever more.
Amen.

—1—

'Father, forgive them; for they know not what they do'

Luke 23.34

The very first word from the cross, the word that we have to make our own, poignantly illustrates the hideous consequences of taking up our cross and following – 'Father, forgive them; for they know not what they do.' Although this prayer of Jesus is missing from a number of important manuscripts, the majority of scholars accept it as genuine to Luke.

By 'them', Jesus could be understood as indicating the Roman soldiers, or even everyone responsible for his execution. But the fact that Luke in his second volume, Acts, makes Peter specifically refer to the ignorance of the Jews in causing Jesus' death (3.17), and puts a very similar prayer into the mouth of the martyr Stephen (7.60), seems to confirm both the authenticity of Jesus' prayer as part of Luke's Gospel and the identity of 'them' as the Jews. Indeed the excision of the prayer from some texts was probably done because later scribes were unable to stomach the notion that the Jews could actually be forgiven. Christian anti-Semitism has a long history, a history resulting from the Church's failure to make the first word her own.

It should though be no surprise to find that forgiveness lies at the heart of the cross. For this instrument of execution is God's expression that people cannot put themselves beyond his love, no matter what bestial and demonic acts they may conjure up. However much people distort their Creator's intention to form them in his image, yet they remain of infinite value in God's sight, the restoration of that image his urgent desire. By appropriating Christ's first word from the cross, we enter into the divine process of re-creation, which frees us from the nightmares of the past and hastens the return of that paradisal kingdom in which the leopard lies down with the kid and children play in safety by snakes' nests (Isaiah 11.6–9).

As the crucified Jesus makes plain, forgiveness is not of the injury or wrong, but of the person – 'them'. Instinctively and uncomfortably we know that the identity of that 'them' is all against whom we have a righteous claim, all whom we will to bring to account for injuries caused to us. Now we understand why before his agony on the cross he taught us daily to pray, 'Father, forgive us our sins, as we forgive those who sin against us'. We cannot in any event expunge the injuries we have suffered. They have had and will continue to have their consequences. But forgiveness enables them to be lived with rather than lived against, releases the victim from their suffocating grip.

These injuries are of course never irrelevant. Sometimes they need to be remembered in order that such evil may never occur again. That is the purpose of the British

Government's decision to commemorate annually the Holocaust by a special day. It reminds us of the bestialities of which humankind is capable and warns against the unwarranted optimism that civilization rids us of our base instincts.

But the requirement to remember has its own internal dangers if it freezes future generations in the past without freeing them to face the future. Christ on the cross takes us further than remembrance: he demands of us forgiveness. For without such forgiveness there is no possibility of that return to Eden, of that creation of *shalom*, peace, which God pronounced as good, and humans in their arrogance despoiled.

By forgiveness we mean two things. In so far as there are those who can know and receive our forgiveness, we free them to enable them to be what God wills them to be. But more important, we free ourselves. Until we can make our Saviour's words our own, our quite understandable hatred of those who have injured us penetrates the very fibre of our being adding to the evil the injury has already caused, and dehumanizing us in ways that those who injured us could never have achieved on their own. Hanging on to hatred, willing revenge, demonizing our adversary – such actions damage us far more than those to whom such feelings are directed. And the worse the injury, the more urgent is the need to forgive.

To forgive is unnaturally difficult; it is not a human instinct, but a divine characteristic. There is little evidence that, despite the New Testament emphasis, Christians are very good at it. But that we fail to live up to our ideals does not invalidate those ideals. Unless we keep forgiveness on our agenda, we neither have any way of dealing with our past nor can provide any hope for the future. There is a terrible fragility about this first word, a fragility we must make our own.

Sometimes Christians have argued that repentance must precede forgiveness. But that is not the way of the cross. Jesus utters his healing words without any precondition. His utterly unconditional act of forgiveness flows from his essential nature as love. There can then be no delay on our part, no excuse. We cannot give ourselves the luxury of waiting on the other's repentance for the longer we wait, the more we become enchained by the situation, frozen in our righteous indignation and adding to that body of evil which ever wills to engulf us. As a friend of mine put it in a letter, 'I cannot imagine that the father of the prodigal son spent his time feeling aggrieved and meditating upon what signs of repentance either of his sons must show before he could begin to consider whether or not he could forgive them.' We may not like the apparently unjust way God deals with other people, but that is the way of love. Without it we as well would perish.

'Father, forgive them; for they know not what they do.' These words of forgiveness were meaningless to those who crucified Jesus. They did not recognize that they had committed any offence. They failed to discern Jesus' nature as the complete expression of God's love, but saw him instead as threatening the basic structure of their distinctive existence as God's chosen people. Consequently in their eyes no blame fell upon them.

This first word then reflects the mind of God at that defining moment when people sought, however unwittingly, to snuff out for all time his irritating and irrational love for them, refusing to acknowledge that their very existence depended on it. But the prayer of forgiveness released the dying Nazarene – released him to die as he was created to die, at one with both God and humankind. So for all, even the crucifiers, he made atonement, became for all time the means of God and his people's mutual and unbreakable embrace.

Forgiveness then is not primarily concerned with justice as we understand it. Indeed the forgiven may be dead or even unaware of the offence committed. Forgiveness is primarily concerned with the release of the injured from his hurt, of stopping dead the chain of injury that would otherwise for ever run on unhindered. It is easy to ridicule forgiveness as weak or foolish, but we know from the cross that that is God's way. In fact forgiveness is no easy way out, but desperately hard to fulfil, which is why we find every good excuse to avoid its practice, even the pernicious appeal to justice.

Unless though we make this hard word from the cross our own, we are in danger of becoming that very force we decry, in danger of becoming one of 'them'. Demonic forces can be equally at home in us fed by the festering sores of unforgiven wrongs. For our concern is not to eradicate those who have done us wrong, rather it is to eradicate wrong itself, and we can and must start with ourselves.

We have then already found with the first word, the word of forgiveness, that the way the world sees things is not how things really are. Nothing could appear weaker than the naked figure on the cross forgiving his executioners, colluding as it were in his own demise. But it is when we are at our weakest, when any opportunity for covering up our nakedness has been torn away, that men and women can assume the natural strength intended in their creation. In responding to the mind of God expressed in the word of forgiveness, we surrender everything on which we might legitimately rely. We recover the glory of our creaturely nakedness.

We knew that taking up our cross would be painful: we were prepared to be stretched in tension, prepared to be pinned by the nails. But how much more painful it is to love those who stretch us, those who pin us. Yet paradoxically once this is undertaken, we encounter a peace, wholeness, at-oneness that transcends all the previous pain and most surprisingly gives meaning and purpose to what hitherto was irrational and incomprehensible. In putting on the mind of God, we see things from a very different perspective; his perspective, as the prophet Hosea recognized:

My heart recoils within me,
    my compassion grows warm and tender.
I will not exercise my fierce anger . . .
for I am God and not man.
                    (Hosea 11.8–9)

If we are to enter into the mind of God, we too must view 'them' with the same divine compassion, the same warmth and tenderness.

Lord Jesus Christ, who in the poverty of your
naked agony
forgave those who crucified you,
release us to forgive our enemies
that we may know that peace, harmony, wholeness
which is your will for us and all your people,
each dependent on your own forgiving love.
Amen.

2

'Truly, I say to you, today you will be with me in Paradise'

Luke 23.43

Having pleaded with his Father to forgive those who have condemned him to death and set about his execution, Jesus is now free to enter Paradise. This term derives from a Persian word meaning park or forest, which was taken over first into Greek and then Hebrew. The Greek version of the Hebrew Scriptures, translated in Alexandria beginning in the third century BC and known as the Septuagint, uses this word for the garden of Eden.

By the time of Jesus, some groups within Judaism had come to believe in life after death, though there were a variety of ways in which this was understood. Some continued to hold the traditional view that the dead, both the righteous and the wicked, descended to Sheol, an underground pit, where they existed in a kind of limbo until the general resurrection and final judgement (1 Thessalonians 4.13–16). Others thought that as the first man and woman had inhabited an idyllic park, so after death the righteous would immediately enter such a paradise. In death the faithful become what they were

15

created to become, citizens of Paradise, residents in the garden of delight, the probable meaning of Eden.

In the second word, Luke accepts this idea of the afterlife, picturing Jesus as completely confident as to his immediate destiny after death. But the second word proclaims that it is not only Jesus who will be in Paradise but one of the crucified criminals too. Unlike his companion, he has recognized the reality of the situation, enabling Jesus to promise him companionship in Paradise. For the second word from the cross is an answer to the thief's plea, 'Jesus, remember me when you come into your kingdom' (Luke 23.42).

How are we to understand the term 'kingdom'? Does this refer to the inscription placed over Jesus' head: 'This is the King of the Jews'? Or did Luke intend by the first word of forgiveness that in Jesus a new rule was breaking in, a kingdom not of this world, but one that offered hope even to this self-confessed criminal condemned to death?

Certainly this would fit Luke's idea of the kingdom elsewhere in his Gospel. This is not understood as some far distant future event, but recognized as even now being realized for those who have eyes to see and ears to hear, those who acknowledge his rule. So Jesus replied to the Baptist's disciples:

> Go and tell John what you have seen and heard: the blind receive their sight, the lame walk, lepers are cleansed, and the deaf hear, the dead are raised up,

the poor have the good news preached to them. And blessed is he who takes no offence at me. (Luke 7.22–3)

In claiming to fulfil the prophecy of Isaiah (35.5–6), Jesus confirms that the end time had indeed dawned, that Messiah's rule was already breaking in, as the lives of those whom he had already freed from whatever enchained them confirmed. Through his acknowledgement of Jesus' kingship, the criminal is to find that he too is freed – to make an identical journey to that of Jesus – that together before the day is over they will both be in Paradise.

It is an astonishing promise. Yet despite anything people may do, it remains on offer to all whatever their condition, for God who is love can will no other destination for those whom he has created in his image. Paradise was our intended destination from the dawn of time. It simply remains for individuals to appropriate the promise, acknowledge the generosity of God. That is both the meaning and necessity of faith.

Like the Hebrews on the edge of the promised land, we have to cross the Jordan to make the promise our own; like the convicted criminal we have to acknowledge Christ's rule, however apparently improbable, in order to enjoy his paradisal kingdom. Always it will involve abandonment of what we have hitherto enjoyed, even if that enjoyment has been less than perfect. Always there will be risk as we embrace the unknown future. The promise of

Paradise could be a cruel hoax. For however much we seem to glimpse Jesus' kingdom breaking in, there can be no guarantee of Paradise this side of the grave. That can only be entered through our final abandonment of all that we are, through death itself.

And what of life in Paradise? We know from the story of the creation of the first man and woman that it was never intended that humans should be idle. As tenant farmers, we are placed in the garden to till it. Our *raison d'être* is to be co-operators with God in the ordering of his creation. But like the first man and woman, we cannot resist the forbidden fruit. We want to 'know good and evil', that kind of knowledge which only God can have. Rejecting our creaturely state, we grasp at divinity. Appropriately the first man's disobedience results in the disorder of thorns and thistles. So it will be for us, chaos always being the inevitable consequence of our attempt to play God.

Our ultimate destination is not then an extension of life here as we know it, but the life for which we were created and have never yet embraced, being unable through our innate hubris fully to carry out the terms of our tenancy, fully to co-operate with God. Yet we shall be as we were intended to be, enabled to do God's will and so enjoy that wholeness and harmony which is the real life that God planned from the dawn of time for every one made in his image and likeness – made to reflect, but not usurp, his glory.

Jesus makes a similar point when questioned by the Sadducees about the nature of the resurrection life in which they did not believe. Citing what was in their eyes the ridiculous case of a woman married seven times, they enquire who will be her husband in the life to come. Jesus replies: 'When they rise from the dead, they neither marry nor are given in marriage, but are like the angels in heaven' (Mark 12.25).

The resurrection life cannot be thought of in terms of life on this planet. It is of a totally different dimension. Marriage is something given to some to help them pass through this world, but our ultimate destiny is to be as the angels, those beings who, freed from all other claims, ever focus on God alone as they go about his business and fulfil his will. That is the precondition of Paradise, the only terms on which it can be enjoyed. In making this second word from the cross our own, we acknowledge that all we will for ourselves is a future in which we concentrate solely on making ourselves available to God, being entirely at his disposal, and so assume our destiny as citizens of Paradise.

If in entering into the mind of God, the first word from the cross daunted us by demanding from us the exercise of his divine compassion, the second should delight us as, now freed from all that inhibits us, we ourselves are embraced by God's warmth and tenderness in the promise of the joy of at last being our real selves.

But the fullness of the real self cannot be found in our

present condition. The thorns and thistles inhibit us from such realization. It is no use hoping like the other criminal for an extension of life here. Nothing would be gained if anyone did take us down from the cross. Paradise can only be reached through taking it up, allowing ourselves to be stretched and nailed, our body pierced. We have to surrender life as we know it in order to embrace life as God intended it. The gospel is not a call to self-preservation but to self-annihilation, an abandonment of all we at present are that we may in future be as God desired, naked and unashamed before our Creator. Paradoxically salvation is not of this world but beyond this world, though it gives meaning and purpose to all we strive to do and be while still in this world. But that doing and being is of necessity provisional; its actuality lies beyond our present reach in the garden of delight where the crucified Messiah alone can take us.

Jesus Christ, as you promised in your impotence to
the repentant thief that he would be with you
in Paradise,
give us such faith that in embracing the
powerlessness of your cross,
we too may find ourselves in the garden of delight
to dwell with you for all eternity.
Amen.

3

'Woman, behold, your son! . . . Behold, your mother!'

John 19.26–7

The third word from the cross poses many difficulties for scholars. The conversation takes place only in John's Gospel; the presence of the women and the disciple whom Jesus loved so near the crucified that they can hear his dying words seems improbable; while it would have been natural for Jesus as head of the family to make provision for his mother's care, why was she not entrusted to his younger brothers? It is with them that she appears after the resurrection (Acts 1.14).

All this leads to the suggestion that, as so often in John, to take the incident at face value is mistaken; rather it must be interpreted theologically. John is not concerned with precisely recording events of long ago, but rather in presenting his contemporaries with his interpretation of the significance of those events. As the Jewish girl Mary gave birth to Christianity, so she as the representative of the old faith is entrusted by Jesus to the representative of the new, the beloved disciple. Israel's destiny lies solely in the recognition of Jesus as the Christ and in membership of his body the Church without whom she has no meaning nor purpose. The Church in her turn, if she is to understand her identity aright, must remember that she derives from her mother Judaism from whom alone she receives her self-understanding.

It is part of John's artistry that this incident at the end of his Gospel complements the story of the first miracle at the wedding in Cana at the beginning of the Gospel. There John tells how water used for Jewish purification rites is transformed into the new wine of the gospel, thereby indicating that the old covenant has given way to the new. It is a miracle in which Mary plays a central part and at which the disciples are present. The two incidents are intended to frame John's Gospel.

But if we are to take up our cross and make the third word our own, we cannot ignore the poignancy of the situation in which it was said nor its natural meaning. For it is in the tragedy of the human encounter of mother and dying son that the cross immediately addresses and challenges us, spells out the awful cost of discipleship, a cost our contemporary Church prefers to ignore.

For today's Church has put the family at the centre both of its ministry and ethical concern. Family services dominate worship, and family life is to be promoted as the desired norm in educating children. Not only does this narrow focus make second-class citizens of the single and the childless, emphasize the failure of the divorced and single parents, and justify the marginalization of those whom society already marginalizes; it also bears little relation to biblical teaching. Jesus so far as we know never married and Paul saw marriage as a second best to be entered into to contain and control human desire for those who 'have not the gift of continency', as the marriage service in the 1662 Book of Common Prayer earthily explains.

It is of course true that Paul was writing in the context of his own times in which the Church believed it was living in the final days, at any moment expecting the return of Christ. It was important that nothing should distract or inhibit the faithful from the urgency of proclaiming the gospel of salvation throughout the Gentile world. Though the Church no longer believes herself to be under such immediate pressure, none the less there does still remain an urgency about the gospel. Every hour is 'now'. Choices are being offered and decisions taken. No Christian ought to allow any other obligation to inhibit their commitment, not even their family.

When he began his controversial teaching in Galilee Jesus rejected not just his family's concern for his safety, but the family itself, announcing to the crowd that 'whoever does the will of God is my brother, and sister, and mother' (Mark 3.35).

Nor were family duties to be allowed to inhibit the absolute demands of Jesus. So scandalously, Jesus told a would-be disciple to forgo that most sacred of all filial duties, the burial of his father, and immediately follow him

(Matthew 8.22) and proclaim the kingdom (Luke 9.60). For his disciples, even saying goodbye to their families was forbidden: 'No one who puts his hand to the plough and looks back is fit for the kingdom of God' (Luke 9.62). Jesus knew that if he personally or his disciples were to exercise their ministries effectively, family ties could make no claims upon them, despite the ancient commandment to honour one's father and mother.

So freed from family duties, Jesus set his face towards Jerusalem and inevitable conflict with the Jewish authorities who would attempt to silence him for good. It is at this point – his mission apparently in ruins as he faces death, yet conscious that he has remained true to the God who had called him to leave the carpenter's shop at Nazareth – that Jesus can consider family obligations.

Stretched on the bitter wood, Jesus is free to express his compassion for the woman who had unwillingly let him fulfil his destiny. He entrusts mother to friend and friend to mother. They are to adopt each other. So with these final worldly dispositions made, Jesus can set about the business of dying.

By taking up our cross and making the third word our own, we acknowledge that we are not excused our proper obligations for those for whom until death we remain responsible, no matter their or our situation, however difficult. But while in this life God blesses us with the gifts of love and affection of family and friends, that love and affection can be enjoyed only in the tension of the knowledge of our ultimate destiny. Inevitably we can only speculate as to what Paradise or being 'like the angels' will mean for us, but taking up one's cross does impose consequences for us, even in the most natural and intimate aspects of our lives. That may not be a popular thing to say, but the third word, like the first, leaves us in no doubt of the apparent harshness of the enterprise on which we have embarked, a harshness which may not only affect us, but, as Mary knew, those who love us too. As old Simeon prophesied at the presentation of the infant Jesus in the temple, a sword would pierce Mary's soul (Luke 2.35). There is no room for sentimentality in entering into the mind of God.

Lord Jesus Christ, as we thank you for the
precious gift
of the love of families and friends,
and pray that we may ever be loyal to their affection,
yet so enable us to fulfil the singleness of our calling,
that no one shall ever separate us from our love
for you.
Amen.

4

'My God, my God, why have you forsaken me?'

Matthew 27.46; Mark 15.34

With the fourth word from the cross found in both Matthew and Mark, we plumb the depths of our endeavour to enter into the mind of God: 'My God, my God, why hast thou forsaken me?', a quotation from the opening of Psalm 22. Deserted by his disciples, stretched in nakedness on the executioners' cross, Jesus finds himself abandoned even by God himself. Having known as none of us can know a perfect intimacy with his Father, he now encounters that most feared of all human states for the believer: godforsakenness. Abandoned at the very moment he needed him most, Jesus must face his death alone utterly uncertain as to whether after all his life had any meaning or purpose – or had he been the victim of a gigantic divine hoax? Utterly gone is the optimism of the immediacy of Paradise; instead he faces the reality of that yawning abyss that opens to engulf both his integrity and his belief.

Yet in those last days things had been so clear. As he deliberately rode into Jerusalem in triumph to fulfil the old prophecy of Zechariah, it really did seem that God's kingdom was at last breaking in, that the prophet from Nazareth was the long awaited Messiah chosen to inaugurate it:

> Rejoice greatly, O daughter of Zion!
>   Shout aloud, O daughter of Jerusalem!
> Lo, your king comes to you;
>   triumphant and victorious is he,
> humble and riding on an ass,
>   on a colt the foal of an ass.
>   (Zechariah 9.9)

The crowds clearly understood what was happening, cheering Messiah on his way. But at the very moment when Jesus was at last being recognized for who he was, God apparently deserted him. In quick succession he was arrested, tried and condemned to death. With indecent haste he was taken out of the city to be hung as a criminal on a cross. There and then, as Job's wife advised her afflicted husband, he could have cursed God and died; he did not and lives. There is nothing suicidal about his death; it is a deliberate and calculated act in which Jesus lets people do their worst – yet, as John asserts, remains in control.

But nor is Jesus the passive suffering servant depicted by the unknown prophet of the exile (Isaiah 53). The Church's identification of him with this poetic figure, an identification not made by Jesus himself, has distorted the significance of the nature of his death. It is untrue to apply to him the prophet's words:

He was oppressed, and he was afflicted,
    yet he opened not his mouth;
like a lamb that is led to the slaughter,
    and like a sheep that before its shearers is dumb,
so he opened not his mouth.

(Isaiah 53.7)

For Jesus does not die in silence. His agonizing cry pierces the demonic darkness of that day. He dies in passion, hurling a question at the absent God, and in doing so preserves the integrity of his faith. For in these last words, which quite clearly depict his utter isolation, he none the less affirms his belief in his Father: 'My God, my God'.

Like Abraham poised with the knife above his only son, Jesus is faced with annihilation – apparently willed by the very God whom he had hitherto implicitly trusted and obeyed. Unlike the patriarch, he has to carry the acceptance of that annihilation through the very jaws of death itself. No ram is caught in the thicket. He has to let himself be destroyed, and the destroyer appears to be God himself. This is the cost of discipleship, what it means to take up one's cross.

We do not know precisely what was the charge against Jesus, but his statement about the destruction of the temple seems to have been crucial. Yet as John indicates (2.21), that temple was his own body, his whole identity and personality, his consciousness as the one sent by God, Israel's long-awaited Messiah. In his bitter reproach to his Father,

Jesus abandons those certainties that had characterized his ministry, and in agnostically embracing death, takes the ultimate risk of challenging the apparent meaninglessness of his life. Paradoxically his own physical destruction, the supreme sacrifice, would make the temple – with its elaborate sacrificial system designed to ensure God's permanent relationship with his people – redundant. So Matthew (27.51), Mark (15.38) and Luke (23.45) all record that at the point of Jesus' death, the curtain of the temple was torn in two. Nothing could now separate God from his people.

Some scholars have held that in quoting the opening words of Psalm 22, which ends in triumphant affirmation of God's purposes, this fourth word should not be interpreted as a cry of despair, but an expression of ultimate confidence in God. But the fact that both Luke and John suppressed this word, evidently understanding it as improper on the lips of Jesus, indicates that it was originally taken at face value and seen as expressing the utter dereliction experienced by Jesus in the face of his apparent desertion by his Father. Even he was not spared that ultimate test of faith – godforsakenness.

Jesus then embraced his death not in suicide, not in resignation, but in passion. In the face of an absent and inexplicable God, he remained true not only to God but to himself too. He was prepared to die with a fundamental question concerning not his but God's integrity on his lips; die as we must all die, without knowing the answer to his challenge. His was a truly passionate act of self-committal, which at the same time appeared as an act of self-destruction, destruction at the hands of the very God in whom he had placed all his hopes. It is also the course that he bids us, his disciples, to follow.

We should not then be surprised if we find this fourth word on our lips as we struggle to make sense of life and find God unhelpfully absent. Faith is risk. There can be no ultimate certainties, not even God's presence, and questions will remain unanswered. To look for any other way than an agnostic expression of faith is to misunderstand the God who wills us to know him, but who at our greatest point of need can appear as the enemy apparently demanding our self-destruction. In that way alone lies resurrection.

Yet the Church today remains preoccupied with self-preservation, the search for a formula that will ensure her survival. That explains why so few can find in her the life-enhancing marks of resurrection. For if we are to make this fourth word our own, we too have to lift the knife, allow our temple to be destroyed. And we must do that in the face of a God who at our point of need remains agonizingly absent, who can in fact only be present again to us through our utter abandonment of our naked, helpless self on the cross we will to make our own.

We know then that we are set on an illogical journey, for throughout his ministry Jesus challenges the presuppositions of the world. It is not the rich who inaugurate the kingdom, but the poor. It is not in power that God's will is achieved, but in powerlessness. It is not those who save their lives, but those who lose them that reflect his nature, lose them alone and abandoned by the very God that in their agony they affirm.

It is then only with the fourth word that the totally uncompromising harshness of our calling becomes apparent. For faith is not something that is expressed in an academic abstract manner; it is something to which one must commit oneself, which demands action; not any action, but passionate action. For faith is passion. Faith is no blind acceptance; it is a deliberate and calculated act in which all is risked, in which total annihilation stares one in the face, annihilation brought about by the very God whom one has hitherto known and trusted, and who now refuses to disclose himself.

Faced with the apparent hostility of God, believers can renounce him and justify their actions by blaming God for letting them down. It is his fault if he is absent without leave and will not explain the inexplicable. That way lies certain death from which there can be no resurrection. It is in faithful impotence among the inconsistencies, confusions and resentments flowing from an apparently indifferent God that his power is manifested, in passion that his rule is realized. In making the agonizing cry of the prophet from Nazareth our own, in recognizing the dimensions of divine powerlessness and willingly enfolding them, we make it possible for our nailed and broken bodies to walk free in a freedom they have never known before, and that we call resurrection.

Jesus, when like you we find ourselves deserted
by God
and facing the inexplicable,
give us the courage to embrace our impotence,
and in our ignorance, but preserving our integrity,
passionately abandon ourselves to your Father.
Amen.

5

'I thirst'

John 19.28

Jesus knows his life is drawing to an end. Exhausted by his ordeal, he appeals for one last act of human kindness. No compassion is shown him. Instead he becomes the victim of further gratuitous torture. In response to his request to quench his thirst, a request for water found only in John's Gospel, the passers by echo the afflictions of the psalmist, sadistically increasing it: 'They gave me poison for food, and for my thirst they gave me vinegar to drink' (Psalm 69.21). Even at the point of death, Jesus was to be shown no mercy.

Significantly John depicts the vinegar being offered on a bunch of hyssop. Hyssop was the herb used for sprinkling the doors of Jewish homes during Passover season in memory of the exodus (Exodus 12.22). He is alerting his readers to the true significance of Jesus' death.

For John adopts a different chronology from the other evangelists, which enables him to see the crucifixion as taking place at the very time the Passover lambs were being slain in the temple. For him Jesus is the true paschal lamb whose death will make redundant the Passover ceremonies. To emphasize his identification of Jesus with the paschal lamb, John introduces the narrative of the Jews' request to Pilate that the legs of the three crucified men should be broken enabling their death to follow swiftly. Their bodies could then be removed before the sabbath. When the soldiers come to Jesus, they find him already dead. There was therefore no need to break his legs. He had been properly sacrificed like the paschal lamb without a bone being broken (Exodus 12.46).

But how are we to lay claim to this fifth word? It would be easy here to concentrate on the bystanders, to note the obscenity of their action. In support is the parable of the sheep and goats described by Matthew as the last of Jesus' sayings before the start of his passion narrative:

> 'Lord, when did we see thee hungry and feed thee, or thirsty and give thee drink?' . . . And the King will answer them, 'Truly, I say to you, as you did it to one of the least of these my brethren, you did it to me.' (Matthew 25.37, 40)

But the fifth word is not a mere plea for compassion: it is of another dimension altogether. Nor does John put this word into Jesus' mouth to make his suffering 'prove' Scripture, as a superficial reading of the text might imply. Rather it marks for John the climax of Jesus' weakness and vulnerability. Like the fourth word, which John omits, the fifth word describes the final state of Jesus' abandonment. Again and again the psalmist alludes to his thirst for God, a thirst inflicted by the very God he wills to acknowledge:

> My strength is dried up like a potsherd,
>   and my tongue cleaves to my jaws;
>   thou dost lay me in the dust of death.
>
> (Psalm 22.15)

> I am weary with my crying;
>   my throat is parched.
> My eyes grow dim
>   with waiting for my God.
>
> (Psalm 69.3)

This fifth word 'I thirst' is even more terrible than the fourth. There is no affirmation of belief, no 'My God, my God'. It is as naked in its degradation as the figure who uttered it.

Those who have known all-absorbing pain or want can understand the fifth word. Nothing else matters but the alleviation of the need, and that need is at that point the only thing that exists, the sum of all reality. Those who have reached the suicidal edge, endured the darkness of their very existence, understand that word. We who are baptized should do so too, for have we not embraced the darkness of the waters that closed above us in order to rise to the new life in Christ. If our faith is to be made real for us again then we too must be prepared to make this word our own. And this will be a continuous process until in our own utter powerlessness the thirst of death claims us in our final descent into darkness, our final act of faith.

It is not the bystanders who should preoccupy us, but the gasping figure on the cross; he who confirms that in his humanity he stands beside us, in his imprisoned dependence that he is one of us. His fifth word should both frighten and encourage us; frighten us in that if we are to make it our own, it means inevitable pain and further rejection; but encourage us in our shared experience that where we are, he has been before, and what he has suffered, we can gloriously claim for ourselves.

But let us return to Matthew's parable of the sheep and goats, for there is a deeper connection with the cry of thirst than the response to need. Of the hungry, thirsty, stranger, naked, sick and the prisoner, the King is asked both by those on his right hand and those on his left: 'When did we see thee?' His reply to both is the same: 'in the least of these my brethren'. In other words, if we are to look for God, it is in the vulnerable that we shall find him. The mystery of the cross is that only through brokenness can wholeness be found.

There is then nothing in worldly terms predictable about God. He is continually the God of surprise. We should not then wonder that it is at our most naked and abandoned, at our point of most acute agony that we are not only nearest to God, but most reflect his nature.

Though we may dread making the fifth word our own, in embracing it in total degradation, divinity breaks through both in us and for us. For it is only when we are deprived of every opportunity for self-reliance, stripped of all pretences and pretensions, become in our powerlessness utterly dependent, that paradoxically God is enabled to show himself in and through us by the use of the very talents he has given us for his service. If we would find God at work, then we need look no further than the vulnerable and the broken, all who have nothing and nowhere to hide, all who can only say 'I thirst', and in their pathetic nakedness learn from them. For as the panting victim on the cross confirms, that nakedness is the very image and likeness of God.

Jesus Christ, teach us not to be afraid to say 'I thirst',

that so being dependent on you alone,

we may be enabled to care for all those who call to us for help,

and who in their brokenness reflect your glory.

Amen.

6

'It is finished'

John 19.30

With the words, 'It is finished' – just one word in Greek – we reach the heart of the gospel. This single Greek word, best translated 'It is complete' or even 'It's done', is not just a statement that Jesus' life is at an end, but an exultant cry of victory. What to Pilate and Caiaphas looked like the final defeat of this troublesome Galilean teacher, the end of the whole irksome affair, was in reality his glorious triumph, the moment that marked the transformation of all things for all time, the beginning of the new age. Victory is won not by the rolling away of the stone that sealed the grave, but by the sixth word and the action that followed it. We do not have to wait until Easter. It is on the cross, that bloodied instrument of torture, that God's rule is assured, that atonement, at-one-ment, between God and humankind is secured.

Do not take the figure down too soon. Ponder both the cost and the victory if you would make it your own.

To the end Jesus remains in control. He proclaims his own triumph before voluntarily surrendering his life. He does not wait for death to claim him, but willingly embraces it. Normally the crucified victim died of suffocation when he was no longer able to hold up his head, but let it fall on his chest restricting his breathing. By bowing his head, Jesus deliberately cuts off his breath. No one takes his life away from him. He gives it to seal the revelation of the nature of the God who created his people and will not let them go, to celebrate that he is love and can be no other, no matter what people may do. In the sixth word Jesus proclaims the completion of the work of incarnate love that he had been sent to do, the revelation of the face of God.

Jesus has shown that paradoxically power lies with the powerless, even in death. However much the powerful try to usurp God's rule, however much the human condition seems hopeless, love, of which the cross is the incarnate symbol, will always win through. That is the gospel. Love is not capable of being defeated for it knows no bounds, cannot even be contained or curtailed by that apparent absolute, death. Love has a life force of its own for it is uncreated, deriving from he who is love, the Creator of all things. Its expression is therefore eternal.

Nor does love ever secure her position by power. Yet too often the Church has forgotten this as – abandoning the poverty of her calling as the community marked by the cross of powerlessness – she has sought to strengthen her status, authority and security in worldly terms, and thereby become a prisoner of the way the world thinks. Inevitably then instead of reflecting love, the Church becomes another instrument of oppression. Happily in every age there have been those willing to make the words of the cross their own, and in the poverty of their spirit given hope – that where brokenness is embraced, wholeness is freed to follow.

All this should encourage us to make the sixth word our own. Even in those agonizing moments of total isolation when life appears to have no meaning nor purpose, when in our all-consuming thirst others give us vinegar to drink, then is the time to have the courage to appropriate for ourselves Jesus' exultant cry of vindication. This supreme act of passion is our faith.

In taking up our cross, we know what to expect. We have no cause to grumble nor complain. At no point have we been misled. The six words we have already sought to make our own provide the blueprint for our journey. In obeying Jesus' injunction to sweat it out on that bitter wood, we freely entered into the mind of God who, as St Paul records, 'did not spare his own Son but gave him up for us all' (Romans 8.32). By our act we offer the world a different way of looking at things, a way in which the power that matters is found in powerlessness, a way that rejects status for service, a way that is not frightened by that sheer naked vulnerability which lies at the core of the cross, a way that gives no thought to security, but revels in the chance to risk all. And we can do this because we have made the sixth word our own. For as St Paul goes on to say in his letter to the Romans:

For I am sure that neither death, nor life, nor angels, nor principalities, nor things present, nor things to come, nor powers, nor height, nor depth, nor anything else in all creation, will be able to separate us from the love of God in Christ Jesus our Lord. (Romans 8.38–9)

Knowing then how things stand, on this apparently bleakest of bleak days in the Christian calendar, the commemoration of the death of Jesus, we have no need to be fearful. There is nothing now that can ultimately threaten or destroy us. Of course what lies ahead can only remain unknown. But we can grip the wood with confidence, for it is both the sign and the reality of our victory.

And if we cannot move legs or arms, if we are stripped of all dignity, exposed in all our nakedness, we know that we are more truly what we were created to be than any previous freedom or self-covering provided. Raised on the cross, we know an exaltation such as no king nor emperor can experience. For all its bitterness, the cross gives us a wholeness, harmony and peace that are beyond human understanding for it marks the point of God's recreation of what he intended for us in the beginning and secured through his beloved Son.

With the sixth word 'It is finished', we become finished too – ourselves in a way we never otherwise could have been ourselves, experiencing in Paul's words what it means to 'obtain the glorious liberty of the children of

God' (Romans 8.21). Of course all of us will still encounter bad moments, foolish moments, dreadful moments. None of us has the ability in this life fully to embrace that naked powerlessness intended in our creation. Constantly we will need to reaffirm our commitment to the only life that is worth living – the life of faithful impotence. Yet every time we are broken by failure we can take heart, for with God all brokenness leads to a wholeness of which hitherto we never dared to dream.

By making the sixth word our own, we ensure that, whatever the future, our lives will not be lived in vain, our integrity is secure, and that with confidence, in our turn, we can bow our heads and leave the rest to God.

Lord Jesus Christ, who yourself went out to embrace death,

even death on the cross,

teach us not to be afraid as those without hope,

but so enable us to risk our lives in the power of your powerlessness,

until, in your wisdom, we too can say, 'It is finished.'

Amen.

7

'Father, into thy hands I commit my spirit'

Luke 23.46

Jesus has maintained his integrity to the end. In the face of an absent and incomprehensible God, he has proclaimed his own victory as, bowing his head, he embraces death. Well may Paul exclaim: 'O death, where is thy victory? O death, where is thy sting?' (1 Corinthians 15.55). Given the nature of God revealed in the Hebrew Scriptures, what follows should not surprise. Love cannot deny love. A ram can now be caught in the thicket. God can speak from the storm.

Luke alone records Jesus' seventh word, a quotation from Psalm 31.5, which we must now interpret as the confident committal of all that he is to his Father, sure in his vindication at his hands. For while in Matthew and Mark, the tearing of the temple curtain follows Jesus' death, in Luke it is the cue for the seventh and final word. Secure in the knowledge that he had fulfilled his mission, that even now his kingdom was breaking in, he breathes his last. There can be no surprise at what follows. Love cannot deny love. On the third day he rose again.

We must, though, hold back from jumping too far ahead. As we commemorate this darkest of days, the anniversary of humankind's final attempt to usurp God by the annihilation of incarnate love, the celebration of the mystery of the resurrection lies in the future. But even so we know what is true for Jesus is true for us too. All those who make the hideous instrument of death their own – stain it with their sweat and blood, form the community of the cross – by their very act become too the community of the resurrection. Love cannot deny love.

By taking the seventh word seriously, making the ultimate surrender of all that we are so that the paschal sacrifice is our sacrifice, we glimpse even now an anticipation of the paradisal life, experience a degree of humanity we never knew before, a nakedness of which we need not be ashamed. To our astonishment through this final surrender of our very being, we find that at last we reflect in some as yet limited measure what we were meant to be; become ever so fleetingly, for we are not yet in Paradise, his image and his likeness. This enables us to see in a way we have not been able to see before – to look at things from a different perspective, the perspective of the citizens of the garden of delight.

But we are still in this world. This means there can be no question of denying our humanity any more than Jesus denied his. On the contrary we are to embrace it even more vigorously by trying to live it as in creation

God intended us to live it, not in devilish hubris seeking to usurp God, but in allowing him to be himself in and through us, his designated image and his chosen likeness.

For the awful truth is that he has no other way of being himself in his world. In the cross, he has shown us the nature of his power. His might lies solely in his sacrificial love, and the present expression of that love depends entirely on us – the community prepared to take up the cross, which alone enables us to be the community of the resurrection. It is at those places and times when in powerlessness the Church embraces the cross that the power of God is manifested, that his kingdom breaks in.

As aided by newspapers and television, we daily survey the conflicts that engulf God's broken and distracted world, are we not led with an ever greater urgency to grasp with passion the roughness of the wood, welcome the nails piercing our raw flesh? As our screens flicker with the obscene images of the whole creation 'groaning in travail' (Romans 8.22), do we not cry out, 'My God, my God, why, why, for God's sake, why?'

But awesome as it is, we know that the answer to the question lies in ourselves – we who are prepared to endure the godforsakenness that surrounds us, whether in the destitute and ravaged or in the over-sated and obscenely satisfied, yet still in the deafening silence maintain our integrity to both God and ourselves. We surrender all that we are with the seventh word, in the belief that love cannot deny love – we are the answer.

Christians then have no alternative but to live out their lives under that sign with which at baptism they were marked. In the very act of marking, we find ourselves stretched on the now sacred and sweet-smelling wood, for our body is his body, his spirit becomes our spirit. We too have been anointed 'to preach good news to the poor . . . to proclaim release to the captives, and recovering of sight to the blind, to set at liberty those who are oppressed' (Luke 4.18). However much the darkness threatens, nothing can extinguish the hope that is in us. For the cross has allowed us to see into the garden of delight, to know our potential, to endure both the agony and the ecstasy that is our present condition. That is simply another way of saying that through taking up the cross we discover both the cost and the joy of being that love which passionately we would make our own.

Lord Jesus, as we have shared in your passion,
making your seven words our words,
enable us by embracing your brokenness
to enjoy with you that wholeness which is
the resurrection life,
and so be partakers of your eternal expression
of love
both here and in eternity.
Amen.

Conclusion

There are no more words. Jesus has forgiven his enemies, expressed his hope in Paradise, made arrangements for his mother, railed at God for his absence, made his last earthly request, boldly gone out to meet death, and surrendered himself triumphant to his Father.

The two thieves still writhe in agony, but the central figure of Jesus is now silent and still, his head slumped forward on his chest, the whole body sagging, all life expelled. There is nothing left but skin and bones, a broken and useless body. Even now in the city arrangements are being made for his burial. For that is all that appears left for anyone to do: reverently dispose of the corpse.

It is different, though, with God. It is in stillness and in silence that he performs his creative work, no matter how lifeless and unpromising the material before him. So it was at the dawn of time when nothing existed but a desolate wasteland shrouded in darkness and covered by hostile waters. God hovered over those waters and said, 'Let there be light' and the whole process of creation began.

So in the stillness and silence that followed the crucifixion, when Jerusalem was engulfed in unearthly darkness, God was again at his creative work. Those who had loved

Jesus and yet deserted him would find that no grave could restrain that broken body, that they could know him as they had never known him before – so much so that they mysteriously became his body, the community marked by his cross, which is also the community of the resurrection.

We have sought to make the seven words of the crucified Messiah our own and so entered into the mind of God, the very way he thought as Jesus expressed in speech and action the fullness of his Father's nature. To know the character of our God, we need look no further than the bloodied wood. In making Jesus' passion our passion, we have recognized that the practice of our faith can be lived out only in faithful impotence. We cannot prove to others who Jesus was, even enjoy that proof ourselves; we cannot control events, but know instead the unpredictability of life, an unpredictability in which God himself can appear as the enemy. We have acknowledged the paradox that his way is the way of brokenness, that it is in powerlessness that his presence is found. Now all we are left with as the darkness engulfs us is the impotent corpse.

Our entering into the mind of God would though not be complete without also making the stillness and silence that followed his words ours too. We shall never have much time for this. The burial party is always soon at hand. The stillness and the silence will be broken and the business that is life will again engulf us. But how it moves on will very much depend on what use we have made of this brief opportunity when words stop and time stands still, when we, like Jesus, allow ourselves to hang lifeless, empty ourselves of all purpose. It is then that God's creative energy can be at work. For having surrendered with that final word all that we are, he can take the emptiness we have embraced and fill it with new life as he did on that resurrection morning.

Despite all the agony of the cross, it is the stillness and the silence that frighten most. We cannot easily accept a situation in which there is nothing there, when everything is without form and void. We want to do something, say something, feel something; even more we want to see something done, hear another, be touched. The waiting seems interminable. There is nothing to hang on to, nothing on which to rely, save our impotent selves bidden to do nothing but remain silent and still.

All this seems unnatural for beings who take it for granted that they were created to be ever active. But this is to misunderstand the kind of activity intended by our Creator. For the form we assume in the silence and the stillness is that state intended in our creation, that original nakedness when nothing separated the man and the woman from their God, a nakedness of which they were entirely innocent. In such a state they were able to co-operate with God by doing his will. That is Paradise.

In the end, the cross is about allowing God to be God. In taking it up, making the seven words our own and then embracing the stillness and the silence, we allow

God to be God in and for us. Broken, emptied, void, he enables us to be as we have never been before, for nothing now stands in his way in realizing himself in and through us. The resurrection is not something that occurred once long ago; it occurred and occurs wherever we allow God the conditions to carry out his creative work, in those who take up the cross and follow into the stillness and the silence that completes its work.

Almighty God, whose Son hung dead upon
his cross,
give us the courage to enter into the stillness and
the silence
that followed his crucifixion,
that you may perform your creative work in us,
so that we may be partakers in your Son's
resurrection
both now and for ever.
Amen.